That Was *Oasis*

Also by Michael McFee

That Was *Oasis*

Michael McFee

Acknowledgments

Thanks to the editors of these magazines and anthologies, for first publishing these poems:

Appalachian Journal: "McCormick Field"; *Cincinnati Review*: "It," "Unbuttonings," "Hydrotherapeutical"; *Cornbread Nation 4*: "Salt," "Pork Skins"; *Epoch*: "Thelonious and Archie"; *Five Points*: "A Hymn"; *Gettysburg Review*: "The Copperhead," "Study Hall"; *Hudson Review*: "Bald Spot"; *N.C. Poem in Your Pocket*: "Erasures"; *New Republic*: "50," "Bibliotaph"; *Poetry Southeast*: "Poultice"; *Shenandoah*: "Bunk," "The Banjo," "Mistletoe"; *Slate*: "Old Newspaper Clipping in an Old Novel," "Holding Hands"; *Southern Cultures*: "Gravy"; *Southern Review*: "Handful of Keys," "Tree House," "Lit"; *Tar River Poetry*: "Street Preacher"; *Threepenny Review*: "Q," "Cigarette Urn," "Saltine," "Tipsy"; *Virginia Quarterly Review*: ":"; *Waccamaw*: "Oasis"

Thanks too to Philip Memmer, who later published "Handful of Keys" and "McCormick Field" as part of my chapbook *Never Closer* (Two Rivers Press, 2005).

Thanks to the College of Arts and Sciences, UNC-Chapel Hill, for a William R. Kenan Leave, which gave me the time to finish this book, and to the University Research Council for a generous Publication Grant.

Finally, thanks to Ross White and Alan Shapiro for helpful advice, and especially to Michael Chitwood, whose prompt and sympathetic readings have improved my poems for many years.

Book design: Anh Bui

for Stephanie McFee

Contents

IV

V

VI

I

Q

U's mate, *O* with a new root,
the one capital letter
which probes below the base line,
here's to the quirky beauty

of its tail, that fluent tongue
stuck from a wide-open mouth,
that elegant half-mustache
parted quickly toward the east,

that antique handle we grasp
to lift up the monocle
of our alphabet's monarch,
that final flourish of the quill.

Erasures

Who knows how many words
I've reduced to mere rubbery static
with the hand that wrote them,
scraping the paper hard until only
a shadowy blankness
was left behind, blowing and then sweeping
smudged eraser crumbs off
the scrubbed sheet to linger in gritty drifts
at the edge of the desk:
changed mind's detritus, second thoughts' debris,
revision's residue,
I gather up a pinch and then toss you
over my right shoulder
for luck, a backwards gesture for language
as yet unrubbed-out.

The Copperhead

Grandmother Ella Zoa
would never have flailed
with the hoe as I did
in my driveway at dusk,
hacking the copperhead
that had dared to slither
its way into the open
for some residual heat
and startled the human
hurrying to convert
garden tool to weapon
with uplifted hands,
protecting all mammals
from that sneaky reptile:
no, she would've calmly
raised the wooden handle
then brought the blade
down, fast, once, clean,
as if targeting a weed
in her vegetable patch,
venomous head severed
from the whiplash body
she'd scoop up draped
over the once-red metal
and toss still squirming
into the viney thickets,
as taught by her great-aunt
when men were blasting
the long tunnel through

old Beaucatcher Mountain
before the Depression,
deep dynamite charges
spooking hidden snakes
downhill into Asheville
where unruffled women
in their narrow yards
deftly dispatched them,
not swearing and striking
bright panicky sparks
from the radiant concrete
by smiting the cold meat
again and again and again,
by chopping that writhing
into bits of raw muscle
that couldn't slip away,
by making the already-dead
as dead as humanly possible.

Salt

That was the taste their country tongues craved,
my parents and their parents and ancient kin:
not sour, not bitter, not funky umami,
not (like us, their spoiled television kids) sweet

but salt, pepper's twin, sugar's quiet cousin
seeping from fatback into simmered green beans
or pinched into steaming dishes by the cook
or flurried hungrily from our grainy shakers.

They'd even salt fruit, fat knife-sliced wedges
of an apple or (better) a juicy watermelon
on the picnic table, that seedy red meat sweaty
with melting crystals: summer in the mouth.

I'd pick up stray grains with a licked fingertip:
Who is the Morton Salt girl? Does she own a mine?
My mother simply laughed and shook her head.
Our blood must have been briny as the Dead Sea.

There are five basic tastes in the human palate;
that salty umbrella girl never really existed—
now I know. Now I watch my sodium intake
as the doctors instruct. But how I crave it.

One day, like my parents and all their parents,
I'll become the salt of the earth, pale seasoning
waking the hidden flavor of the family plot
until I too lose my savor, forgotten underfoot.

Cigarette Urn

Little zen desert
in a shallow bowl
raised on a pedestal
to passing hand-level,
you used to attend
tuxedos and gowns
in the crystal lobby,
waiting for them
to extinguish half-
finished unfiltereds
into the fine sand
later cleaned and raked
into elegant swirls:
now you must loiter
by the dark back door,
guilty butts jabbed
into ashy gray grains,
brown filters angling
upwards like legs
stuck in a nightmare
whose bodies of smoke
long ago disappeared.

Old Newspaper Clipping in an Old Novel

It flutters to the table
but leaves behind a silhouette,
a yellowish-brown rectangle
its newsprint pressed into
the front endpapers for decades,
an inkless stain, inverse bleaching,
the author's obituary scissored
by dutiful librarian or fan
casting a shadow bookplate,
its grave a greasy window
we can't quite see through.

II

Saltine

How well its square
fit my palm, my mouth,
a toasty wafer slipped
onto the sick tongue
or into chicken soup,

each crisp saltine a tile
pierced with 13 holes
in rows of 3 and 2,
its edges perforated
like a postage stamp,

one of a shifting stack
sealed in wax paper
whose noisy opening
always signaled *snack*,
peanut butter or cheese

thick inside Premiums,
the closest we ever got
to serving *hors d'oeuvres*:
the redneck's hardtack,
the cracker's cracker.

Poultice

Her little boy bee-stung, yelping,
Mom tapped a cigarette from her pack

and peeled back its flimsy paper
with a long chipped pinkie nail

then pinched some loosened tobacco
into her mouth, a dainty plug

she chewed until it was just wet,
gently lifting out with her tongue

a cud, a brownish wad, a gob
she plastered to his swelling bite

and spread until the red was hidden,
telling her sobbing son, "Don't touch,"

its unlit darkness drawing out the fire,
its poison canceling the angry bee's.

Gravy

Meat grease, flour and water, stirred till smooth—
it's what my forebears ate, if they were lucky.

It's what my mother ate, those hard dark years
she worked at a sawmill way out in the mountains,
learning to live on cigarettes and coffee

and cold biscuits raised from the dead by gravy.

Now and then she'd cook a little for us,
something to moisten and darken and quicken

the bowls of bland white rice or mashed potatoes
I'd shape into a cratered volcano
whose steaming lava overflow improved

everything it touched on my dinner plate.

Good gravy's not an afterthought, a dressing,
a murky cloud masking a dish's dull prospect:

whether poured from a Thanksgiving china boat
or a black iron skillet in Bloody Madison,
it's the meal's essence, where flesh meets spirit,

where fat becomes faith, where juice conveys grace

as red-eye, giblet, sausage, faithful sawmill—
whenever I think of those savory names

and the times I've poured or ladled or spooned
then mixed and dipped and sopped up their elixir,
not wanting to waste a single filling drop,

my mouth starts making its own thin gravy again.

The Banjo

Plunking the rusty washtub bass
was simple, tautening or relaxing its rope
so that a few thumping notes
rose or fell at the floor of a bluegrass tune.
And it wasn't that hard to squeeze
some buzzing chords from the budget guitar

when the rehearsers took a break
to step outside the basement for some cokes.
But my tall cousin was the only one
stubborn and patient enough to teach himself
to play, fiercely as Scruggs, the banjo:
he'd stand perfectly still, head tilted forward,

watching his long pale hands flashing
as if they weren't part of his body anymore,
the right one with slipped-on picks
speedily crawling among the twanging strings
stretched over the full-moon belly,
the left one racing along sharp steel wires

up and down that skinny neck
until his finger pads started bleeding again,
fresh calluses splitting as he played
"Foggy Mountain Breakdown" one more time,
my cousin only wincing slightly as
the music scarred and healed his flying touch.

Pork Skins

Before we get down to the bacon,
the chops, the tenderest of loins,
long before slow conversions
to sausage or barbecue or country ham,

there's this pesky question of skin
to be gotten past somehow,
a muddy rind that must be dealt with;
and since our hungry ancestors

ate all of the swine but its squeal and tail,
somebody somewhere sometime
took sharp knife to scraped hide
and cut it into bite-sized rectangles

he cooked down then popped up,
curling salty parchments
he chewed and dryly swallowed,
pronouncing them (choking a bit) good:

and so they were, and so they still are,
these little fried clouds
filling my mouth with the crunchiest
hint of pig, a noisy meringue

that needs no sweet pie for flavor,
its shining airy cells dusting
my chest and fingers with palest gold,
the apotheosis of the epidermis.

Handful of Keys

1.

Fats Waller meant the piano's,
the ivories he astonished in his 1929 solo
as if playing all eighty-eight at once,
big left hand striding, big right hand swinging.

But I mean all these office keys
spilling with a rich clinking from my cupped hands
into a cardboard box on my boss's desk

like hundreds and hundreds of ancient amulets
with long toothy snouts.

2.

Somebody stole the master key,
raiding the locked strongboxes of our offices.

These surrendered keys smell
like the fingers that long pinched and turned them,
like the pockets and purses that held them safe,
these little swords that once secured
us and our wordy vaults—

a moist brassy stink, grimy, vaguely human.

3.

Mr. Fortner, the ancient janitor
at our valley school south of Asheville,
kept a gleaming hoard
of used keys in the furnace room, that fiery cave.

He carried a passkey called a *skeleton*
that could open any door.

Later, we'd learn
the sexual metaphor of key and lock,
of blade slipped firmly into well-oiled cylinder
then turned until something opened . . .

And we'd learn that sometimes a key is just a key.

4.

At heaven's locked gate,
St. Peter waits with the keys to all the doors
I ever opened in my mortal life

except for one,
the one I must find, the very key to paradise,
disguised to look like the others
whose entered rooms I can no longer remember.

I wish I could melt this useless metal down
and make the master key of master keys,
the key to the City of God:

is that Fats I hear inside,
finishing "Handful of Keys" to angelic applause?

5.

I stand outside the same old office door,
fingering my new key.
Nothing will have changed inside, and yet
I can't enter a locked room
without looking around, checking things out.

Were Fats' hands playing the coffin lid
when they lowered him into the Harlem earth,
still great with music?
My my my, one never knows, do one?

I trace the grooves and serrations,
the freshly-carved still-crisp descending line
my lock alone comprehends.

Our hands are the keys that will open
just one more song.

III

Bunk

"That's just a bunch of *bunk!*"
I hollered at my windbag teenage cousin
teasing out tales about my sister
there on the side porch's spongy slanted floor,
describing her raw adventures
with twins in a rowboat out on Beaver Lake.
I was too young, too American
to say *humbug, claptrap, balderdash, twaddle*;
I might have known to call it
baloney but hadn't yet learned *guff, hogwash,*
or what his ripe lies were:
bullshit, horseshit, dogshit, just plain old *shit.*
And I had no clue that *bunk*
came from the same Carolina mountain county
where I continued shouting it
at my kinsman multiplying empty words
about how the Vance boys
lost their paddles and had to drift all night
taking turns comforting sis:
he wouldn't sit down and shut up any more
than voluble Congressman
Felix Walker, who defended an ill-timed oration
on the House floor in 1820
by saying he was "only speaking for Buncombe,"
to the constituents back home
and not to his colleagues who'd been debating
Missouri's slave or free status.
And so his self-serving pointless speechifying
entered the language as *bunkum,*

immortalizing my native place as a synonym
for *piffle*, *poppycock*, and *rot*,
nonsense, horsefeathers, flapdoodle, hooey, hokum.
All I knew to do, in 1963,
in my nine-year-old righteous brotherly rage,
choking on the purple prose
of Asheville dusk and the story's moonshine
and the gall of my slick cousin
filibustering to hear his own foolish voice,
was stick with the loud sentence
adults pronounced to end their arguments:
"That's just a bunch of *bunk*!"

Tree House

A fort hung in midair,
a penthouse clubhouse,
a private boys' heaven
lookers-up could merely
behold the floor of:
that's what we wanted
to build in pine woods
next to Jason's house
with plywood scrounged
from construction sites.
But then his cop dad,
a lanky volatile man
with Aqua Velva cheeks
and thinning Brylcreem hair
(greaser comb-splatters
coated his bathroom wall),
caught us drawing plans,
so our tree house retreat—
a laid-back attic room
to hang out in, a nest
hidden in swaying limbs—
became his latest project:
he quadrupled the size
and bought fresh lumber
and spent hot weekends
in his basement workshop
perfecting the pieces
before assembling them
(pounding and swearing,

his empties drifting down
like metallic pine cones)
much higher than we boys
could ever have managed.
"I hate that old bastard,"
Jason spat, glaring up,
and I said, "Yeah, me too,"
though secretly I admired
the triple-lock trap door
and BB gun embrasures
and rope ladder escape
of what was now a bunker,
a lofty fallout shelter.
We never did play up there
but his officer father
would climb the nailed rungs
(too far apart for our legs)
and stand in his crow's nest
and smoke Dutch Masters
deep into many nights,
keeping watch in the dark
high above the lawful sleep
of family and neighbors,
haunting the canopy
with his cigar's steady glow
and smoke blown at stars
and crisp manly redolence
of combing and shaving,
borne on the needled breeze.

Oasis

Its very vowels
were an exotic blossoming
in the desert of lessons
about Israel in exile,

a mantra I mouthed
while stepping into
the framed pious painting
and onto a dromedary

that swayed us away
through blistering heat
toward three date palms
shading a pool

where an unveiled beauty
waited with water,
calmly lifting a bowl
to my cracked lips

as I drank deep, staring
into her cool green eyes:
o that was no mirage,
that was *oasis*.

Study Hall

When Sandra Pope draped
one long long leg over the other knee, rocking it
till the stocking's warning track
darkly snuck out from under her tight miniskirt,
none of the boys around her
considered how the flesh surrounding the hinge
that let her calf lift and bounce
and fall was already spoiled with a spidery bruise.
None of us knew that the rivers
on that map would stay flooded the rest of her life
as they had for the dour teacher
who wore support hose and rubbed swollen veins
and kept frowning at our corner.
All we could see were Sandra's never-ending legs
measuring out the shortest hour,
the quietest period in the history of that school,
as she slowly uncrossed them
with a nylon hiss and tugged at the stubborn mini
and deliberately rehung knee
over knee, the steady pressure of being a coquette
impressing its blue birthmark
a little deeper as the circle of scholars around her
resumed its furtive study
of the physics of that arc and swing and sway.

Holding Hands

After weeks of yearning
half-taps and near-grasps,
my sweaty palm found hers
and we made a leaky basket
of our interlaced fingers
and that was it, hallelujah,
finally we were holding hands
in public, we were shaking
sideways on a visual contract
everybody could understand,
I was hers and she was mine,
the two of us had begun
becoming one clasped flesh,
now we were happily coupled
from the supple wrists down,
we were carrying the pet
with two backs between us
as if we'd never before
squeezed another human
in such a meaningful way,
as if she had never seized
her tall anxious mother
when first learning to walk
or cross the lethal street,
that firm grip saving her,
as if I would never clutch
a dying father's calluses
in cardiac intensive care
and feel our shared pulse,

the mutual prayer of blood,
as if she and I would never
tire of each other's touch
and try to figure out how
to escape this embarrassing
collision of crinkled skin,
this padded cage of bones,
these too-long-opened fists
before somebody passing by
mistook for love our resigned
inability to quite let go.

It

I know what all boys want, her father said,
a Navy vet, a life insurance man,
and he was right, I wanted it real bad

though I wasn't sure exactly what it was,
only that his cute smart only daughter
and I felt something stirring as we sat

side by side night after night on the sofa
in the dim living room nobody used,
listening to stacks of classical music

to improve our minds (her mother's idea)
while we necked and petted and half-listened
for his heavy footfall from the kitchen,

the signal to separate and straighten
before his reddened face passed by the door,
a florid moon enraged by what it saw:

his girl, this clueless boy, the pungent it
he hadn't felt himself in many years,
stinking up the place like Rachmaninoff.

What could he do, but make another drink?
What could we do, but hide our eager hands
inside each other's clothes once he was gone

and kiss till our cells hummed like cello notes?
I never thought I'd be a jealous father
saying his line to my own flesh and blood

or to her suitors when they came to call
or to myself, patrolling the empty halls—
knowing what all boys want, and missing it.

IV

Tipsy

She was only lightly lit, not
sloshed or smashed or plastered

but tipsy, a little bit tripful
and bumpish and aslant, feet on floor

and words in loosened mouth
not crashing together but brushing

chummily, wobbling, almost
toppling before righting themselves,

a couple of drinks rouging
her pale cheeks one sheet to the wind

but not two or three, not yet
tipsier or tipsiest but just plain tipsy,

laughing, leaning on friends
more than usual, her eyes glistening

as she told another tilted story
with a beginning, a muddle, and no end.

A Hymn

They always said they went to church
at least to give their restless kids
traditions to rebel against.
And that's what every last one did.

They thought it would be easy to
make Sunday mornings fun again.
How tedious those brunching hours.
How very flat the weekend's end.

And so they started sneaking back,
not for the earnest fellowship
but for that holy moment when
they stood together, hip to hip,

and sang aloud a hymn they'd missed,
not for the antiquated words
but for those joyful noisy layers
of harmony they sometimes heard

as her breathtaking alto line
and his approximated bass
and all the mistimed heartfelt parts
surrounding every opened face

hung heaven in that mortal air
and echoed in their emptied throats
long after they were headed home,
long after the Amen's held notes.

Street Preacher

Most of his sermon is lost
as he jogs our suburban neighborhood
barking fitful holy words:
today I could barely make out *salvation*
and *holy ghost* as he passed,
a small black man in a blank white t-shirt
and blue jeans and tennis shoes,
bearing something in a plastic shopping bag—
his Bible, maybe, the source
of an obscure verse he keeps fulfilling
by making daily circuits
and preaching to the streets he runs along,
his calls puncturing the air
with no response except from all the dogs
who hear him coming far off,
the sharp notes of his tenor shouts afflicting
or blessing their hungry ears
as they bark or howl or cry till he passes,
heavy legs headed elsewhere
with the message only he or God hears whole.

:

It never stops flashing on my car's clock,
this heartbeat punctuation between hour and minute:

this twin star pulsing in the local sky,
its snakebite part of a minor constellation's myth:

this luckiest domino, whose dot-dot code
keeps spelling out *light* against the deepest darkness:

this cross-section of a blinking equal sign,
its lines parallel to infinity, if only I could see that far.

Lit

Where do they come from, the butts in our yard,
spent ammo of cigarettes slowly smoked down
to sunny brown filters mottled as birds' eggs,
flimsy bible paper and tobacco ghosted away

by neighbors, strangers, unimagined stalkers
tossing their exhaled minutes in our direction,
used-up hyphens fallen out of conversation,
cottony seedpods that will never yield a crop;

or are they from my late mother and father
circling the house, flicking ashes into the bushes,
looking into the lit windows at what they made,
at what cigarettes helped them leave behind,

a son coming home from a bar where he watched
his fellow drinkers convert themselves to clouds,
mixing fire and water until they were happier,
until they'd managed to forget the day's insults,

the night's to come, the smoking loitering kin
always lighting up again, always wanting back in?

Thelonious and Archie

1.

Before they were known as "Monk" and "Ammons,"
they were just two down-east North Carolina kids

born poor on the wrong side of town, or on the farm,
who grew up tall and smart, with big strong hands

and a knack for playing hymns by ear on the pianos
in their mothers' churches, the soundtracks for Amens.

2.

Thelonious was a teen when he hit the gospel highway
as part of the house band backing a lady evangelist,

a family friend and faith healer named Reverend Graham
whose hard-charging nickname was "The Texas Warhorse."

They were on the road for several years: later, all he'd say
about it was, "She preached and healed, and we played."

3.

Archie, eight years younger, played for local revivals
and services, a skinny Depression boy sowing seeds

of song, his red hair a soft flame over the keyboard.
Onboard in the South Pacific, in a Navy-gray chapel

on the other side of the world from Whiteville, he'd try
to tease hymns from pianos also always out of tune.

4.

Maybe they liked not being part of the congregation,
not having to go forward to be saved or healed.

Maybe they liked watching the pretty girls come down,
confessing, sobbing, praying, glistening with sweat.

Maybe they liked how even the crudest music and verses
could lift people out of themselves for a few minutes,

5.

connect the believers to something truly exalted,
beyond notes or words yet wholly grounded in both

and in the body, in sweet feet and fingers and mouth.
Nearly half a century later, playing hymns on his upright

one chilly Ithaca fall night, Archie said, "*This* is where
my poetry comes from—forget that Transcendental shit!"

6.

Nobody pays much attention to the piano player
whose job is to listen to and watch the revival preacher

and keep each holy marathon moving steadily forward,
playing the white and black keys as if they were souls

trapped in flesh moving toward a much-desired climax,
never losing the urgent heartbeat or halting the flow

7.

of foursquare song unless the gesturing evangelist
needs a dramatic pause to drive God's message home

to sinners who must choose heaven or hell tonight,
for now is the appointed hour, even so come Lord Jesus,

the pianist's poised hands waiting to undertake
their pilgrimage to an earthly paradise far from here.

8.

"Sphere" may seem like a middle name he made up
to sound more hip, but Thelonious inherited it,

his mother's father's first name and her middle one,
its nothing-square-about-it jazzy 3-D geometry

rooted in the family genealogy in Rocky Mount,
a town (despite its name) nowhere near real mountains.

9.

"Randolph" was a bland middle name, like most are:
the poet in print went initialed, as stalwart A. R.,

though everybody called him "Archie" in person.
He did name one poem *Sphere*, a book-length sentence

linked by colons as Monk's tunes hinge on silences,
the music of bluegreen planets that never cease moving.

10.

Monk stops pounding the piano in *Straight, No Chaser*,
rises from his bench again and starts spinning slowly

in a mute dance that could be ecstasy or madness,
a dizzy evangelist (eyes closed, listening to the spirit)

who believes that you must save yourself first and last,
convert your being to an emptied brimming space.

11.

Ammons strides down the long tall hall to class.
He knows that he must, yet again, tell his students

not to use the tired old word "God" in their poems
but he also knows that every poem is a kind of hymn

to the human urge to craft the holiest language,
as every hymn is a song of praise to itself, to words

12.

and music creating worlds that others can also enter,
and be moved by, and love, and remember, even once

the psalmists return to dust, their hands no longer
moving over ready keys, their names nothing more

than faded letters on spines, though what they made
lives on in the air, in their lines scoring page after page.

V

Unbuttonings

Slowly, he undoes himself
in the bedroom's twilight—

right hand/left cuff, thumbing
the wrist's thick strings;

left hand/right cuff, rubbing
the long-shackled skin;

both hands/collar buttons
no longer tethering the tie;

left hand/wrinkled placket,
lifting it and squeezing

seven faux-bone disks
through tight buttonholes

starting at cinched throat,
unfastening downward—

and misses the lidded tin
full of unmatched buttons

his grandmother always kept
near her heavy black Singer,

how rich he felt plunging
his flared fingers deep inside

or pouring a clinking heap
in the middle of her bed

when everybody was gone
and finding exotic ones

like bright foreign coins,
sighting through threadholes,

a landlocked boy biting them,
sniffing where they'd been.

Mistletoe

Doctor Winter
discovers this tumor
high in the overarching oak,
un-shot-down, unreachable,
its stormcloud planet
stuck to an outermost branch,
parasitic darkness
under which only the dead
will ever be kissed.

Bald Spot

1.

At first it's just a rumor,
a gossipy joke between mirrors,

nothing more than a hint
of bare forest floor
starting to gleam through what had been
a dense canopy.

2.

Lord, you know I did not pray
for this monastic tonsure
emerging like a slow-motion shearing,

this skullcap of scalp
gradually bared, a bull's-eye for heaven.

3.

Did I scratch the crown of my head
too much, feigning thinking?

Or did I sleep too often and too long,
pillowfriction and dreamthrashing
thinning my already-thin hair?

4.

Pale pate,
you loom, you glow dully
as a moon veiled by wispy clouds
or a failed halo.

And you keep on rising, rising
like a boulder long-hidden
at the bottom of a lake being drained by drought.

5.

Everybody has a soft spot
for a soft spot, a baby's holey cranium,
but nobody really wants to fondle
this middle-age fontanel.

6.

I could try to cover it
with my rueful hand, with a ball cap,
with too-long feathery neighboring strands
meticulously combed over,

with hirsute chemicals from can or jar,
with plugs transplanted
as if reconstructing a lawn blade by blade,

but nothing can halt its spread
except death, the smooth Prince of Alopecia.

7.

Or should I just shave everything off,
a dinosaur egghead
whose waning brain is about to hatch,

a terminal humpty dumpty
about to fall?

8.

God never answers, of course,
he merely continues
rubbing the top of the unbowed head
of his once-obedient pet.

9.

I dream I wait alone
on a treeless ridge, at the edge
of a bald deep in the mountains,
burned clear by lightning centuries ago.

As I wait for the Indians
to finish crossing the clearing and find me,
I envy their long black hair

flowing thickly behind them,
how utterly it absorbs the last of the light.

50

Sealed into this leaky
barrel of myself,
I brace against staves
creaking and aching
as the bitter river
races toward a Niagara
thundering dead ahead:
can my rattled skeleton
survive unpulverized
the pandemonium
of that tumbling plunge,
touch bottom then surface
to yellow slickers lining
a tour boat's deck, waving?

Hydrotherapeutical

Late-day sunlight bouncing off the surface
of water troubled by kicks and strokes and turns

swims the walls and ceiling, a psychedelic effect
I enjoy as I sprawl alone in this hot tub,

training a powerful jet on my aching neck
and shoulder and back and hip and calf and foot,

listening to the lane swimmers patiently
plow back and forth over there in the adult pool,

slowly laying open the same long slippery furrow
that quickly fills behind them every time,

small waves complicating the dazzle overhead,
the light show I savor as I shift and wish

that this gym served chilled champagne
so I could toast the brothers Jacuzzi who built

the first whirlpool bath, which led to this pleasure
awaiting me at the end of every workout

when I choose not to do laps but simply
to sit and let underwater geysers massage my flesh

as the face-down swimmers continue their work,
pushing forward like dull ploughshares

slicing through soil, leaving a shallow trench
in which they hope to plant a long and healthy life

or at least a decent chance of dying less soon
than some pale guy surrounded by bubbling water

whose currents are stirred by a switch and a motor,
not the steady propulsion of legs and arms:

I could defend my hydrotherapeutical behavior,
explain how these airy pressurized streams

help remove lactic acid from tired tissues,
open up blood vessels, improve endorphin flow,

but really I just like the way this heated swirl feels
and how it and the trippy sunlight pattern

seem to cheer my heart, suspended like a fat seed
inside the age-bruised fruit of a body

still buoyant for now, not yet sown in a row.

Bibliotaph

Bury me with my books.
Slip one under my head:
a satin pillow's much too soft
for such a rigid bed.

Bury me with my books.
Open some on my chest,
their pages shadowing the heart
beginning its long rest.

Bury me with my books,
tossed in until the hole
is filled with words instead of dirt
and I am like a mole

happy to stay hidden,
not needing light to see
that paper heaven made by hands,
the books that buried me.

VI

McCormick Field

"What a ballpark! What a beautiful place to play!"
—Babe Ruth, 1931

1.

I watch the old man keeping score
a few rows down, a few seats south
here at the new McCormick Field,
each pitch, each out, each hit, each run
recorded in those blue boxes
whose empty frames his hand will fill,
a system my late father tried
to teach me forty years ago
in the original ballpark
when he sat by me marking up
another Asheville Tourists game.
The old man licks his pencil's point
the way my dad would always do.
He doesn't eat, he doesn't drink:
he watches closely, then he writes
until each at-bat's finally done,
part of a neatly-tallied sum.

2.

Up narrow Biltmore Avenue toward the park,
up the faulty sidewalk from the after-hours lot,
up the gray stone stairs, footworn as a cathedral's,
up (in dad's hands) to the barred ticket window,

up the concourse crowded with hunger and thirst,
up the section ramp, a loud cramped tunnel,
up the steep concrete steps to our own two seats:

fold down, sit down, look down on the field
glowing before us like an immaculate garden.

3.

For years, my father-treasurer kept the books
for the postal credit union, spreading out
those wide black ledgers on our kitchen table,
each page a grid of pale red and blue ink
ready to be filled with columns of numbers,
additions, subtractions, subtotals, balances.
He'd pencil figures and then punch them
on the massive Remington Rand machine,
pulling its cocked arm for noisy hours
to see if his accounting had worked.
It's no wonder he loved to keep score,
to enter and update and save all the data,
each player's position assigned a digit
from 1 to 9, pitcher to right fielder,
each play a letter or abbreviated cluster:
BB, HBP, DP, 1B, SB, PH, RBI, K.

I was far too impatient to practice
the shorthand dad used those summer nights.
But he'd still let me mark his scorebook
when one of our Tourists went deep
and I got to write HR, then draw four lines
to connect the dots of the bases,
then color the infield solid with my pencil
until it shone, a soft black diamond.

4.

The field was named for Dr. McCormick,
Asheville's first resident bacteriologist,
who was so appalled by the plague of flies
swarming the livery stables and streets
that he started a campaign in 1904:

"Swat That Fly!" It started with local kids
paid by homeowners to kill *Musca domestica*
as it paused rubbing its filthy legs together,
then spread quickly across the country,
a grassroots public health success

that earned him a nickname: "The Fly Man."
And so every batter who swats another fly
and every fielder who runs to haul it in
continues that extermination mission
begun a century ago right here in town.

5.

We'd find the best view of home plate
under the grandstand roof, behind the screen,
so his scorebook wouldn't get wet
and we wouldn't be blindsided by line drives

and we could watch the pitches break
or sink or rise or hiss past the batter
trying to protect the strike zone,
that phantom pane of glass, that grave in air,
as the ump's fingers sprouted strikes
on the right hand and balls on the left, outs
clenched with a fist, his fingertips

resting lightly on the catcher's shoulder
as he leaned forward, waiting for
the next approaching blur he had to call.

Dad said the only better seats
were in the press box perched up on the roof,
that heaven right above our heads

where writers and announcers watched the game
and quickly turned it into words.

6.

Thomas Wolfe was a tall batboy
for the Skylanders in 1915,
loping toward home
to fetch the cast-off lumber.
"Hurry up!" the manager yelled.

Tom loved how the plate
was simple as a kid's drawing,
a single-gable white house
every hitter wanted to get back to.
"Son," the catcher growled, "move it."

7.

We went so often, father and son,
our programs' lucky numbers won stuff:
a case of Royal Crown Cola
whose heavy beveled bottles clinked
all the way to our trunk,

whose wooden crate we never did return,
twenty-four square holes
in which I displayed all the balls I'd collected;
free oil changes, dry cleaning, burgers;

and (most exotic of all) a string tie,
a bolo made in San Antonio,
its slide a flat red baseball
with white feather stitches and TOURISTS
pressed into the sharp-edged plastic.
Why did they reverse the colors?
I wondered while sliding that bloody circle
up and down the dark blue cords,
the metal-tip aglets clicking as I walked.

8.

The old man sharpens his pencil
with a pearl-handle pocket knife
like the one dad used to carry,
cedary shavings at his feet
like peanut shells crushed under mine.

9.

The fireworks started early
one Fourth of July:
my nose exploded in a sudden bleed,
my father quickly stanching it
with his handkerchief and surprising pressure,
jamming a piece of folded paper
up under my top lip

and making me lie down across his lap,
head hanging back into the aisle,
legs stretched out across a couple of strangers
who never stopped watching the players.

And dad never stopped scoring them,
my chest his desk
as I studied the rafters and the light standards,
the sparrows bearing scraps of food
and the swooping bullbats clearing the buggy air.

10.

Heilman in right is a blur, kicking weeds:
thanks to a couple of green pitchers
who won't even make the team,
his Detroit Tigers are losing 18-14
to the hometown Asheville Skylanders

in their brand-new park's official debut—
wooden grandstands packed to capacity,
low rail fences lined with dark-suited men
tilting their black hats forward
to keep the cold sun out of their eyes.

April 3, 1924, not a single leaf on a tree
in this black-and-white panoramic photo,
not an ad in sight, the only sign
a motto crowning the roof: ASHEVILLE—
THE PLAYGROUND OF AMERICA.

Cobb, the bitter Peach, player-manager,
fumes in center with hands on hips;

Manush waits in left for this exhibition
to be over, it doesn't count for anything.
.403, .358, .334: that's what they hit last year

but still finished second to the Yanks.
One day these three will be in Cooperstown,
bronze plaques shining from the Hall's walls,
far away from the leather-lung hillbillies
whose grass they water with major-league spit.

11.

"Great game, Magoo, too bad
you can't see it!"
I lacked the guts and lungs
to insult the umpires,
every ticket holder's right
my father once told me.
"How can you sleep
with all these lights on, blue?"
All around us, red-faced men
would cup hands around mouths
and megaphone abuse
on those crooked judges,
their heckling sometimes echoing
off the encircling hill:
"Hey ump, the eye doc called,
he's fixed your glasses!"

"*Asses*,"
came the longed-for after-jeer.

12.

Later in '24, the Skylanders
(too many letters to stitch across a chest?)
were quietly rechristened the Tourists,
acknowledging the many summer visitors
to The Playground of America

but also the players, coaches, and umps
who hoped they were merely touring Asheville,
sojourners soon to be in the majors,
not on their way down and out of pro ball
or stuck in this mountain-girt town for good.

13.

The scoreboard flashes H, not E:
the old man shakes his silver head.
A home-field ruling, undeserved,
but he erases and corrects
then adds an asterisk and note,
his unofficial marking-down.

14.

Dad knew all the ballpark regulars—

the blind black guy who watched each pitch
loudly on his transistor radio,
always a second or two behind the action,

the retired band director Mr. Denardo,
pained by the bad canned music
but beaming in his box as he conducted us,
holding the ascending notes of "old . . . ball . . . game"
till everybody collapsed, laughing,

Struttin' Bud Shaney, star pitcher
for the '28 Tourists, best team ever dad said,
later the crafty groundskeeper
who could sculpt and pack and water the basepath
so it favored the Tourists that night
or hindered the visiting Phillies or Braves—

and they knew him, another local
who'd played the sport well once upon a time
and prayed for a son and got lucky
and brought the boy here when he was a tiny baby
and ever since so that he could learn baseball
by simply being inside it,
a language they shared without speaking

as they sat side by side, night after night,
never closer.

15.

The Bambino died in Asheville:
that was the rumor in April of '25
when the Yankees trained into town
and Babe fainted in the stucco depot
in front of a mob of star-struck fans

and was rushed off in an ambulance
and didn't leave town with the team
after they won at McCormick Field.
The *Citizen* reported he had "the flu"
but the evening *Times* ran a picture

of The Sultan of Swat flat in bed,
hands folded helpless on his big chest,
which helped fuel the wildfire gossip
that "the flu" really meant he was dead,
a victim of his unchecked appetites,

struck down in the blue mountains
celebrated for their healthfulness . . .
Six years later, Ruth and the Yanks
were back, he and Gehrig homering
high over the steep right-field bank

into the crowd that couldn't get seats.
I wish I'd asked my dad if he was there.
This time, the over-the-fold photo
showed Babe winking at the camera
as he kissed a cute young V.A. nurse.

16.

The mound's a low mountain
on the mowed plain of the field,
an ancient volcano
erupting strikes through Dock Ellis
and visitors like Nolan Ryan,

but I was 12 in the summer of '66
so I loved offense and Bob Robertson,
our moody slugger with a swing
so compactly fierce
that when he caught one on the sweet spot
his bat rang the night like a tuning fork,
that deep sound thrilling our seats' wood
and my startled heart
and my rising father's tingling palms
and the trees beyond the left-field fence
waiting for his towering blow
to finish its re-entry in leafy darkness.

17.

"Take . . . me out to the ball . . . game,"
we stood and sang, seventh-inning stretching,
the only time my old man and I
ever lifted up our voices together in song.

"Buy me some peanuts and Cracker Jack,"
the kids would shout, and the drunks
would lift their last beers and laugh
and toast, "I don't care if I never get back!"
as we shared our true national anthem—

not the unsingable "O-oh-say can you see"
crackling overhead before the first pitch,
a few fans mouthing its baffling lines faintly,

my dad's hat over his heart, his smiling lips still,
both of us waiting to cry, "Play ball!"

18.

Just north of the park was Valley Street,
the "Niggertown" where nervous whites
taking a shortcut to First Baptist
told their kids to lock the car doors
against idle Sunday morning porchsitters.

Back in the forties, black fans could stroll
down the long hill and fill McCormick
to cheer for their Asheville Blues,
playing Negro Southern League games there
whenever the Tourists were on the road.

I never saw Colored fountains or bleachers
but as I root-root-rooted for Willie Stargell
the air around me shifted uneasily.
Now Valley Street is a brief cul de sac
ending behind the county courthouse and jail.

19.

Dad wrote his proud surname in the lead-off spot
the summer I was a Babe Ruth All-Star shortstop
and we played one afternoon at McCormick Field.
I ran from the dugout in my Sealtest Dairy uniform
(leaping the fresh base path lime) to the very spot
where Davey Concepción had starred the previous year,
then warmed up with the South Buncombe infielders

before removing my red cap and facing dead center,
watching the star-spangled banner too hot to wave
as I tried to calm the butterflies by praying hard
God, please don't let the ball be hit my way, please

and it wasn't, I fielded no chances in two innings
and struck out in my one at-bat, but no matter,
I'd played on the field where my heroes had played
though no picture survives to prove I ever did
and dad's record vanished with all his scorebooks.

20.

He marks the Tourists as he marks
the Sand Gnats, River Dogs, Catfish.
I wonder: does he save those sheets,
or does he keep such faithful score
for its own sake, for the pleasure
of noting every lit movement
for a few hours, for a few months,
for who knows how many decades?
—A crisp objective pencil stroke:
three outs, another inning done.
The old man flips his book and waits.

21.

In college, I swore off sports as bourgeois
though my father still asked me to join him
at the park, when the Tourists were in town,
or in the den, watching cable baseball
the way we once watched the Game of the Week,
laughing at Dizzy Dean's corny malaprops,

but I said No thanks, and so he sat alone
with the close-ups and the instant replays,
falling asleep as Atlanta lost again.

22.

The last time I saw the original park
was in a New York theater, summer of 1988,
a cameo in *Bull Durham*.

Asheville skyline in the background,
Crash Davis drives his Mustang convertible
up the hill, past the stone staircase,
through the right field gate and out of sight.

McCormick was then the oldest baseball field
in the minors, fifth oldest in America
after Wrigley, Fenway, Tiger and Yankee Stadiums—
a dank antique, cramped and dim and haunted,
like the national pastime.

Three years later, they razed its rickety wood
for a concrete and brick "neo-traditional facility."

23.

My dad and I study Ted Williams
finishing his sweet lethal swing,
torso twisted but balanced
between bent right leg stepping forward
and left leg dipping slightly at the knee
so that back foot lifts on its ball
as it pulverizes the dirt,
front arm parallel to swung bat
lifted clean and flat over his shoulders.

We stand side by side, looking up
at this painted basswood statue
of the Splendid Splinter homering,
father and son sharing baseball again,
making their long-delayed pilgrimage
to the Hall of Fame in Cooperstown.
Dad cocks his head and turns my way
and I expect him to appreciate
the finer mechanics of hitting
as demonstrated by the follow-through
of his favorite batter of all time—
No. 9, The Thumper, The Kid,
dark keen eyes lifted, still on the ball—
but instead he asks a question
that stuns me into disbelieving silence,
this white-haired ancient touching my arm:
"Now, just who is that, son?"

24.

May 27, 2004: it's Thirsty Thursday
at the new park, rebuilt on the original site,
and dollar-beer attempts to start the Wave
keep collapsing before it can undulate
all the way around to the bleachers,
and Ted-E Tourist, the bear-like mascot,
is dancing lewdly on the home dugout roof,
and the lesbian couples stand to cheer
when the enormous P.A. voice booms,
after some inter-inning mock Sumo wrestling,
ATTENTION: NO SMOKING IN THE STANDS,

but the old scribe ignores it all,
updating numbers until the next batter steps in.

25.

I don't know how the afterlife unfolds,
but on that cold March day my father died
at St. Joseph's, a couple of blocks south
of the original McCormick Field,
spring training scores already brightening
the hospital TV above his bed,
I hope he made it to that beautiful place,
the doomed ballpark that Ruth himself admired,
and lingered in the shady stands a while.

I hope he made his way out to the infield
then climbed the unraked mound, that circle of dirt
he'd focused on for almost seventy years,
and peered back in toward home, a ghostly zone,
waiting for the dark-blue-suited figure
to gesture that the game could now begin,
waiting for his catcher to give the sign
(one index finger pointed toward the ground
where his body would vanish in a few days,
under the outfield where nobody plays),
waiting for his teammates' scattered chatter
and whistles to pierce the wide air behind him
before he started his delivery,
the first of many pitches in the nightcap.

26.

He stays until the final out,
records it calmly, 5 to 3,
then closes the cardboard covers
and slips the sharpened pencil snug
inside the metal ring binding.
Wincing, the old man rises stiff,
picks up cushion and umbrella,
passes me on the sticky steps
and disappears into the crowd
high-fiving tonight's victory,
the scorebook tucked under his arm,
a clear accounting of the game
that could be read by anyone
(a fan, player, sportswriter, coach)
who understands his steady marks
and loves the always-shifting stats,
the unforgiving truth they tell.

27.

It's beautiful the way this bright field fills
a lofty little valley between hills,

how perfectly they cup the outfield arc
with viney banks and trees, a natural park

or amphitheater for the timeless play
we watch to end another summer day.